THREE PRINCIPLES
STRATEGY & TECHNIQUE BOOK

*A collection of tools, strategies
& techniques for well-being,
love & resiliency*

**COMPILED BY AMIR KARKOUTI
INSPIRED BY SYDNEY BANKS**

THREE PRINCIPLES
Strategy & Technique Book

Copyright © 2018 by Amir Karkouti
All rights reserved. This book or any portion thereof may not be reproduced or used in any manner whatsoever without the express written permission of the publisher except for the use of brief quotations in a book review.

ISBN-13: 978-1986161701
ISBN-10: 1986161706

Printed in the United States of America

First Printing 2018